Pretty like Jamaica

COLOURING BOOK

Opal Palmer Adisa

Illustrated by Wayne Powell

Based on the book by the same name.

All rights reserved. No part of this publication may be reproduced, stored in a retrieval system, or transmitted in any form by any means, electronic, mechanical, photocopying, recording, or otherwise without the prior written permission of the Publisher.

Published by CaribbeanReads
ISBN: 978-1-953747-28-0 (Paperback)

Copyright 2023 Opal Palmer Adisa
Illustrated by Wayne Powell

Kathryn is Pretty like Jamaica
Read the book to find out more.

Kathryn lives in Jamaica. Here she is with her dog, Brutus.

Granny is Kathryn's grandmother. Granny calls Kathryn Precious. Granny enjoys crocheting.

Kathryn splashing at the beach.

Granny and Brutus on the shore watching Kathryn as she has fun in the sea.

Kathryn and Granny playing checkers.

FIND THE WORD "PRETTY"

How many times can you find the word PRETTY hidden in this puzzle?
Hint: Look for it spelled forward, backward, and diagonally.

Y	T	P	R	E	Q	P	Y	T	T	E	R	P	R
T	P	C	L	T	E	Y	Y	Y	S	P	R	C	E
T	T	K	R	P	R	E	T	T	Y	E	P	Y	E
E	A	Q	P	A	Y	T	T	E	T	P	Y	T	P
R	D	R	Y	P	E	V	Y	T	P	T	A	T	Y
P	U	E	D	R	W	T	Y	R	T	T	E	E	P
Y	Y	P	P	E	T	A	R	E	E	Y	Y	R	R
D	R	P	F	E	T	P	R	E	T	T	Y	P	E
R	E	Y	R	P	P	P	Q	S	Y	Y	P	Y	T
P	K	P	P	L	R	D	A	T	T	T	R	Y	T
Z	L	S	P	L	A	E	T	L	L	T	E	P	Y
O	Y	C	C	O	L	E	T	L	L	E	T	L	T
Y	Y	E	P	O	R	L	L	T	L	R	T	S	C
A	K	R	Y	P	R	E	T	T	Y	P	Y	D	Y

I FOUND IT _____ TIMES!

Kathryn and Brutus chasing after the goats.

Mister Joe's goats eating Granny's flowers.

Kathryn's aunt Mavis visits and gifts
Kathryn a wooden sculpture.

Kathryn is sad sitting in front of the barrel of things her mother sent her. She misses her mother.

Kathryn is excited to speak with her mother on the phone.

Kathryn's mother lives and works in America.

Kathryn loves to read.

Brutus keeps Kathryn's company while she reads.

Granny crocheting in the living room.

Kathryn, Georgia, and Miss Jess, Kathryn's mother friend. Kathryn will travel to America with them.

Kathryn and Granny pack for Kathryn to go to her mother. They are sad to be leaving one another.

Kathryn's mother sends a locket with a picture of Kathryn and her when Kathryn was a baby.

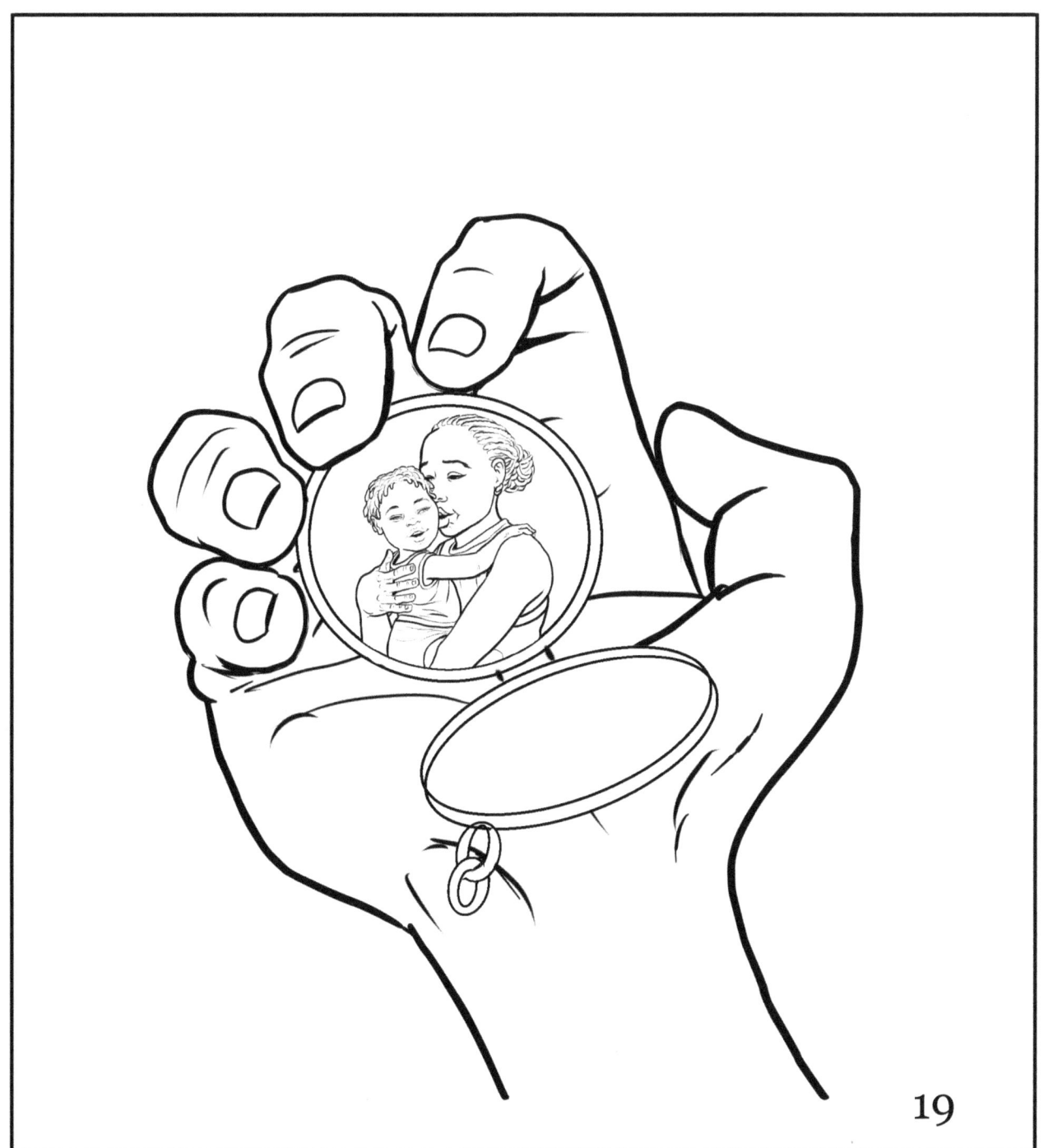

Kathryn's friends at her good-bye party.

Granny, Kathryn, and her friends at her send-off party.

Kathryn and Granny hug goodbye.

Kathryn on the plane with Miss Jess and Georgia.

Kathryn is so nervous, she feels her heart beating like a drum.

Kathryn, Georgia, and Miss Jess going through immigration in New York.

Georgia holding on to Kathryn's hand.

Miss Jess with her luggage.

At last Kathryn sees her mother, her brother Patrick, and sister Janice. They are happy to be reunited.

Kathryn's mother looks her in the eye and tells her she is pretty like Jamaica.

HELP KATHYRN FIND HER MOTHER

Kathryn needs help to get to her mother.
Help her through the maze.

LOCATE THE AIRPORTS

Show Kathryn where all airports are in Jamaica.
Write the location of the airports on the lines below.

Name of Airport   Location on Map

Sangster International Airport, Montego Bay   _____

Norman Manley International Airport, Kingston   _____

Ian Fleming International Airport, Ocho Rios   _____

PRETTY LIKE JAMAICA

Oh No! Pretty Like Jamaica story is all out of order.
Write in the numbers 1-8 to put in the correct order.

SPOT THE DIFFERENCE

Can you spot eight differences between these pictures?
Circle as many missing things in the picture on the bottom as you can!

DRAW THE GOAT

Mister Joe's goat is having a bite. Copy him square by square and draw your own picture.

LET'S FIND THE WORDS

Y	T	P	A	U	N	T	M	A	V	I	S	P	R
T	P	C	M	I	S	T	E	R	J	O	E	C	E
F	T	K	R	P	R	E	T	T	Y	E	P	I	E
R	A	Q	P	K	A	T	H	R	Y	N	E	S	P
L	D	R	Y	P	M	V	Y	T	P	T	A	N	Y
A	M	E	R	I	C	A	Y	R	C	T	E	A	J
C	Y	P	D	E	E	A	M	A	E	Y	Y	N	A
I	R	P	F	N	T	E	Q	A	A	J	H	A	N
A	E	Y	A	Q	N	A	Q	M	Y	B	G	Y	I
M	K	L	P	T	P	D	S	E	T	R	R	Y	C
A	P	S	L	L	R	M	Y	L	L	U	A	P	E
J	Y	P	C	O	L	I	X	L	L	T	N	L	T
Y	Y	E	P	O	F	L	C	G	L	U	N	S	C
P	R	E	C	I	O	U	S	K	D	S	Y	D	Y

1. America
2. Anansi
3. Aunt Mavis
4. Brutus
5. Granny
6. Jamaica
7. Janice
8. Kathryn
9. Mama
10. Mister Joe
11. Patrick
12. Plane
13. Precious
14. Pretty

35

ANSWERS

FIND THE WORD "PRETTY"

HELP KATHYRN FIND HER MOTHER

LOCATE THE AIRPORTS

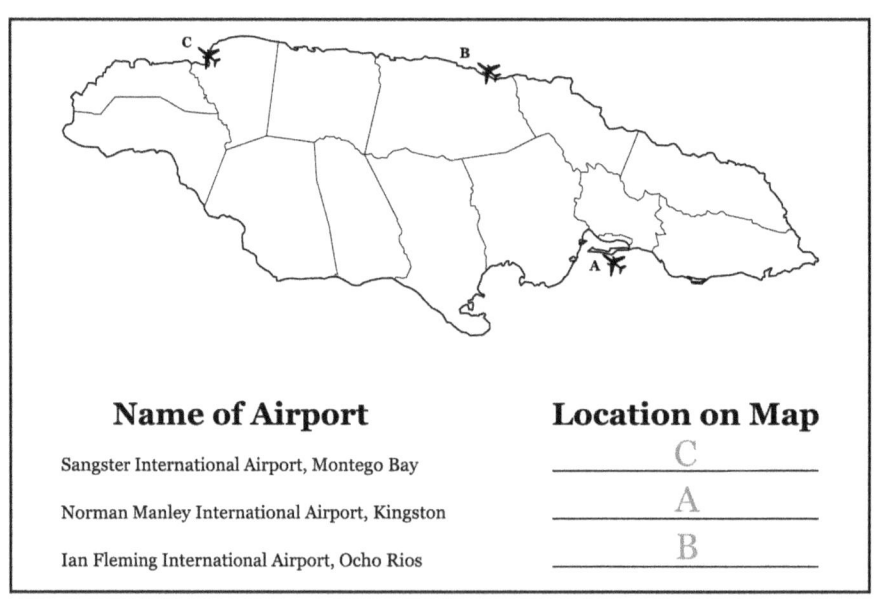

Name of Airport	Location on Map
Sangster International Airport, Montego Bay	C
Norman Manley International Airport, Kingston	A
Ian Fleming International Airport, Ocho Rios	B

ANSWERS

PRETTY LIKE JAMAICA   SPOT THE DIFFERENCE

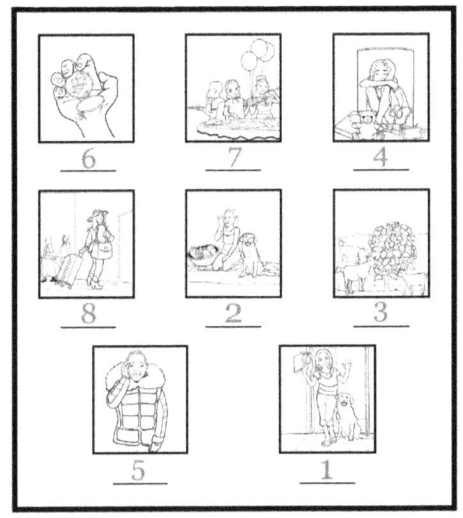

LET'S FIND THE WORDS

Y	T	P	A	U	N	T	M	A	V	I	S	P	R
T	P	C	M	I	S	T	E	R	J	O	E	C	E
F	T	K	R	P	R	E	T	T	Y	E	P	I	E
R	A	Q	P	K	A	T	H	R	Y	N	E	S	P
L	D	R	Y	P	M	V	Y	T	P	T	A	N	Y
A	M	E	R	I	C	A	Y	R	C	T	E	A	J
C	Y	P	D	E	E	A	M	A	E	Y	Y	N	A
I	R	P	F	N	T	E	Q	A	A	J	H	A	N
A	E	Y	A	Q	N	A	Q	M	Y	B	G	Y	I
M	K	L	P	T	P	D	S	E	T	R	R	Y	C
A	P	S	L	L	R	M	Y	L	L	U	A	P	E
J	Y	P	C	O	L	I	X	L	L	T	N	L	T
Y	Y	E	P	O	F	L	C	G	L	U	N	S	C
P	R	E	C	I	O	U	S	K	D	S	Y	D	Y

www.ingramcontent.com/pod-product-compliance
Lightning Source LLC
Chambersburg PA
CBHW041427040426
42444CB00022B/3486